DUMBBELL HANDBOOK

WRITTEN BY

Michael Jespersen
Andre Noel Potvin

EDITED BY

EXPERT: STRENGTH TRAINING & GENERAL FITNESS
Andre Noel Potvin
      M.SC., C.S.C.S., CES

EXPERT: STRENGTH AND CONDITIONING & FITNESS
Bill Luke
      Ph.D., C.S.C.S., Registered Kinesiologist

EXPERT: STRETCHING & GENERAL FITNESS
Nikos Apostolopoulos
      BPHE, NCCP-L3, AACA, AAA, ACSM, IASP

GENERAL EDITOR
Michael Jespersen

COPY EDITOR
Karl Thorson

ASSISTANT EDITORS
Jon Kromhoff, RMT and Linda Jespersen, RN, BSN

Twelfth Printing
(revised September 2004)

Published 2002
Productive Fitness Products Inc.
2289-135A St.
Surrey, B.C. V4A 9V2

For quantity discounts please call toll free:
1-888-221-8833
or write:
Productive Fitness Products Inc.
P.O. Box 2325
Blaine, WA 98231-2325
or e-mail
info@productivefitness.com

Visit our Website: www.productivefitness.com

Jespersen, Michael, 1962-
  The great dumbbell handbook

  ISBN 0-9696773-1-6
  1. Dumbbell. 2. Weight training. I. Thorson, Karl. II. Kromhoff, Jon. III. Title.
GV547.4.J47 1996   613.7'13   C96-910605-X

TABLE OF
CONTENTS

Introduction	4
Weight Training Safety Tips	5
Body Diagrams	6-7
What You'll Need	8-9
Accessories	10-11
How to Set up Your Program	12-15
Stretching	16-20

Dumbbell Exercises

Shoulders

Upright Row	21
Shoulder Press	22
Standing Side Raise	22
Shoulder Shrug	23
Seated Incline Deltoid Raise	24
Screwdriver	24
Pec Minor Punch	25
Lying Single Arm Flyes	26
Standing Bent-Over Flyes	27
Bent-Over Flattener	28
Front Deltoid Raise	29

Rotator Cuff

Side Lying Neutral with towel	30
Side Lying with Arm Braced	31
Prone External Rotation	32
Incline External Rotation	33

Chest

Bench Press	34
Lying Pullover	35
Flyes	36

Back

Bent-Over Lateral	37
Bent-Over Row	38
Deadlift	39

Biceps

Alternating Hammer Curl	40
Standing Bicep Curl	41
Concentration Curl	42
Incline Bicep Curl	43
Incline One-arm Preacher Curl	43

Triceps

Seated Tricep Press	44
Kickback	45
Overhead Tricep Press	46

Forearms

Wrist Curl	47
Reverse Wrist Curl	47

Legs

Squat	48
See-Wall Squat	49
Split Squat	50
Lunge	51
Side Squat Lunge	52
Seated Calf Raise	53
Standing Calf Raise	54
Walking Heel Raises	55
Standing Hip Flexor	56

Core

Two-Arm Dumbbell Crunch	57
One-Arm Dumbbell Crunch	58
Bridge with Dumbbell	59
Reverse Leg Lift	60
Pointing Dog	61

Other Products	62-64

INTRODUCTION

What often stops us from starting or following through with an exercise program is the time and inconvenience involved. Getting to the gym, waiting in line for equipment, and working out in a crowded area is often so discouraging that we don't follow through with our exercise program.

For about the cost of an annual health club membership, you can set up your own mini-gym with a set of dumbbells and a simple exercise bench. The space required for such a gym is minimal, only taking up a few square feet. Moreover, using dumbbells is a great way to strength train because the workout is as good, if not better than using a series of expensive machines. The best part about strength training with dumbbells is that <u>ANYONE CAN DO IT!</u>

Some of the other benefits from strength training include:

- decreased body fat. By increasing your metabolism, strength training increases the number of calories you burn on a daily basis, even while resting.

- stronger bones. Having stronger bones helps to prevent osteoporosis and other bone diseases, while preventing fractures as well.

- improved lymphatic drainage. Your lymphatic system is responsible for removing the toxins in your body. Weight training stimulates the movement of lymphatic fluid.

- increased self confidence. Being and feeling stronger helps to relieve anxieties and fears, while giving you a certain assurance in everything you do.

- improved body image. Aside from seeing your muscle size and density increase you will find yourself standing straighter, with your shoulders back and head upright.

- decreased fatigue. Your stamina will increase and you won't tire as easily.

- faster metabolism. The faster your metabolism, the more efficiently your body will burn fat, digest, and absorb dietary nutrients, while decreasing the amount of fat storage.

- increased motility. This is the speed with which food passes through your digestive system. The less time food spends sitting in your digestive tract the better.

Too often, strength training is thought of as an extreme form of exercise, when in fact it is likely to be one of the most important factors in achieving better health.

WEIGHT TRAINING
SAFETY TIPS

✔ **Always warm up before you start a workout.** Try to do a total body warm-up before you start training. A good example of a total body warmup is using a rowing or skiing machine. It is especially important to warm up the specific muscle groups you are going to be using. A warm-up can be as simple as performing the specific exercise at 25% to 50% of the weight you normally lift at very high reps.

✔ **Use proper posture.** Maintaining proper posture will greatly reduce chances of injury and maximize exercise benefit. When standing, always keep your feet shoulder width apart. Do not lock your knees; it puts an unnecessary strain on them. Keep your back flat and straight, making sure not to twist or arch it in order to complete an exercise.

✔ **Use proper form.** Focus on only working the muscle groups intended for the exercise you are doing. If you feel strain elsewhere you may need someone to critique your exercise motion or reevaluate the amount of weight you are lifting. Keeping proper form also means lifting in a smooth fluid motion. Know when your muscles are too tired to keep going.

✔ **Breathe properly.** Never hold your breath during any part of an exercise. Holding your breath may cause severe intra-thoracic pressure and raise blood pressure leading to dizziness, blackout or worse! The rule of thumb is to exhale slowly on exertion and inhale on the return part of the exercise.

✔ **Stop training if you feel pain.** If you feel pain during a specific exercise stop immediately. Any continuation may aggravate an existing injury. Reevaluate your routine to make sure you are doing a proper warm-up. Decrease the amount of weight you are lifting.

BODY
DIAGRAMS

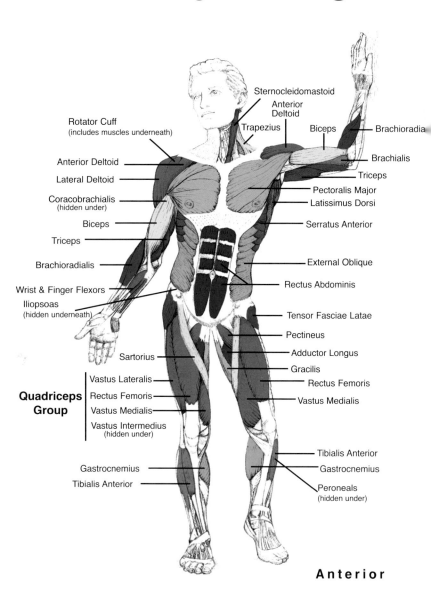

Rotator Cuff
(includes muscles underneath)

Sternocleidomastoid

Anterior Deltoid

Trapezius

Biceps

Brachioradia

Anterior Deltoid

Lateral Deltoid

Coracobrachialis
(hidden under)

Biceps

Triceps

Brachioradialis

Wrist & Finger Flexors

Iliopsoas
(hidden underneath)

Brachialis

Triceps

Pectoralis Major

Latissimus Dorsi

Serratus Anterior

External Oblique

Rectus Abdominis

Tensor Fasciae Latae

Pectineus

Adductor Longus

Sartorius

Gracilis

Rectus Femoris

**Quadriceps
Group**

Vastus Lateralis

Rectus Femoris

Vastus Medialis

Vastus Intermedius
(hidden under)

Vastus Medialis

Tibialis Anterior

Gastrocnemius

Gastrocnemius

Tibialis Anterior

Peroneals
(hidden under)

Anterior

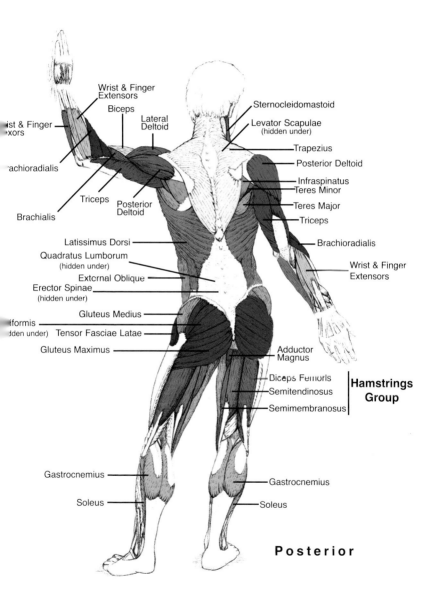

Wrist & Finger Extensors

Biceps

Lateral Deltoid

ist & Finger xors

achioradialis

Triceps

Posterior Deltoid

Brachialis

Sternocleidomastoid

Levator Scapulae
(hidden under)

Trapezius

Posterior Deltoid

Infraspinatus
Teres Minor

Teres Major

Triceps

Brachioradialis

Latissimus Dorsi

Quadratus Lumborum
(hidden under)

External Oblique

Erector Spinae
(hidden under)

Gluteus Medius

iformis
dden under) Tensor Fasciae Latae

Gluteus Maximus

Wrist & Finger
Extensors

Adductor
Magnus

Biceps Femoris

Semitendinosus

Semimembranosus

**Hamstrings
Group**

Gastrocnemius

Soleus

Gastrocnemius

Soleus

Posterior

WHAT YOU'LL
NEED

HEXAGON DUMBBELLS

Hexagon dumbbells are normally sold by the
pound and can vary considerably in price. Hexagon
dumbbells range in weight from 1 lb. to 150 lbs. and
increase in 5 lb. increments after
15 lbs. When purchasing a set
of dumbbells, only purchase up
to a weight you can manipulate
without too much difficulty. Then as you
feel confident to lift more weight, you can
purchase the next heaviest weight. Hex dumbbells are probably
the most desirable type of dumbbells because of their low cost,
ease of use, and compact size. Most dumbbells have knurled
handles to improve your grip. Use weight training gloves if you
are concerned about your hands becoming too rough.

or ADJUSTABLE DUMBBELLS

These are plate loaded handles, to which you can add 1.5 lb.,
2.5 lb., 5 lb., 7.5 lb., and 10 lb. plates. Remember when purchasing plates to get multiples of 4 to balance out both dumbbells. There are two basic types of adjustable handles: either
with a spinlock mechanism or with spring collar clips. These
handles are more economical than the fixed weight variety
because you can change the weight each time you do a different exercise. The main drawbacks to these dumbbell handles is
they are bulky, awkward and you may need to change the
weight each time you do a different exercise.

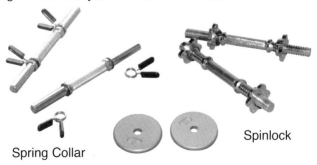

Spring Collar

Spinlock

or POWERBLOCKS

An alternative to the traditional hex dumbbells, The PowerBlock system is especially convenient if space is a concern. The PowerBlock system consists of a core weight with a neoprene handle and a series of interlocking shells to add more weight. Depending on the system, weights can range from 3 lbs to 125 lbs at increments of 2.5 lbs or more, again depending on the package purchased.

PowerBlocks are available at most Exercise Equipment Stores. Ask the salesperson for details on the different options.

and a FLAT TO INCLINE BENCH

A Flat to Incline bench is essential for doing a proper dumbbell workout because it allows you a range of movement which is difficult to duplicate with anything else. This bench is designed so that when you are lying on it you can bring your elbows below your chest level. The front seat should be adjustable upwards to prevent you from sliding off the bench when set at the incline position. When exercising, always set the backrest to an upright position to support your back if you are in a seated position. For instance, when performing a set of shoulder press exercises, make sure the backrest is set in the vertical position. A good Flat to Incline bench should be easy to adjust, made of 10–11 gauge steel, with 8 lb high density rebond foam and naugahyde covering.

ACCESSORIES

1) EXERCISE GLOVES

The two main reasons for using gloves are to protect your skin from becoming rough or calloused and to reduce the stress on finger joints. The leather padding of the gloves will protect your skin from the knurled handles of the dumbbells. Gloves will also help to dissipate the pull of the weight which may cause ligament damage to the delicate joints in your hand and fingers.

2) WEIGHT LIFTING BELT

Belts are normally not necessary when using dumbbells. You may purchase a belt if you feel you need extra support in your lower back. There are generally two types of belts: leather and velcro. Leather belts can be uncomfortable and stiff until they are broken in, whereas velcro belts are comfortable immediately. Velcro belts can also be adjusted to your exact waist size whereas the leather belts can only be adjusted to the next set of buckle holes.

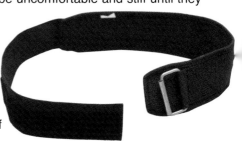

3) STRAPS

Straps are used for lifting heavy dumbbells. The strap wraps around your wrist and comes out over the palm of your hand. You wrap the strap around the dumbbell handle until the weight is supported by your wrist and not your fingers. Straps can be effective when doing certain exercises such as the Bent-Over Row or Shoulder Shrugs.

4) DUMBBELL RACK

A dumbbell rack is definitely an asset for keeping your weights organized. Depending on how many weights you have you can either get an upright rack or a two tier rack. The upright variety usually holds up to 6 pairs and the two tier can hold more depending on the size of the weights.

5) EXERCISE MAT

These mats come in different sizes, but the most common size is 2' x 4'. Some of the different fillers for mats include chip foam, durafoam, and trocellen. Chip foam is the cheapest filler and tends to break down quickly, whereas durafoam and trocellen are likely to last much longer. Durafoam is softer and less expensive than trocellen, but very suitable for stretching and doing floor exercises on.

6) PLATEMATES

When hexagon dumbbells reach 15 lbs., they increase in 5 lb increments thereafter. Often an increase in weight of five lbs. is too great, especially when you fatigue within the desired number of repetitions. PlateMates offer an excellent solution; by simply attaching a platemate to each end of the dumbbell, you can increase the weight in a smaller increment. The increase can be either 1.25 lbs. or 2.5 lbs. depending on the size you select. PlateMates use super strong magnets that attach to the ends of the weight, making them quick and easy to use. PlateMates are available at most exercise equipment stores or by calling 1-800-877-3322.

How To Set Up A
PROGRAM

1. ESTABLISH GOALS

Begin by setting specific and realistic goals. Ideally, set a long term goal and then set a series of short term goals toward the attainment of the long term goal. Once you have made the commitment to see your goal through, list exactly how you will attain this specific goal, including the number of workouts/week, type of activity, time of day for workout, and how you will incorporate this into your weekly schedule. For instance, if you want to increase your overall strength by 50%, record your beginning and your most recent level of strength.

> Week 1
> Chest press: 12 reps @ 15 lbs
> Week 12
> Chest press: 12 reps @ 20 lbs

Simply divide the most recent figure into the beginning figure and subtract 1 to get the percentage increase in strength.

> 1) 20lbs ÷ 15 lbs = 1.33
> 2) 1.33 - 1 = .33 or 33%

Your increase in strength is 33%.

REPETITIONS, SETS , AND WORKLOAD
Repetitions are the number of times an exercise is done consecutively without rest. One complete series of continuous, consecutive repetitions is called a Set. Workload refers to the amount of weight used in working a particular muscle or muscle group.

Look to see what changes in your lifestyle you will have to make to accommodate the new program. From both a motivational and safety perspective, it is a good idea to track your progress each and every time you workout. A training diary can help keep your workouts consistent and efficient.

2. COMPONENTS OF A SUCCESSFUL STRENGTH TRAINING PROGRAM

FREQUENCY

Exercise each muscle group 2-4 times per week. Allow a minimum of 48 hours rest for each muscle group worked. If you are doing a total body workout, three training sessions per week, performed on every second day, is adequate.

DURATION

A workout session should take anywhere from 30 minutes to 1 hour to complete.

RANGE OF MOTION

Moving through a complete range of motion (ROM) allows the muscle to stretch before contraction and increases the number of fibers being recruited. This produces maximum contraction and force. By working the full ROM flexibility will be maintained or even increased.

SPEED OF MOVEMENT

Strength training movements should be slow and controlled. Do not use momentum to complete an exercise. Momentum puts unnecessary stress on tendons, ligaments, and joints and does not develop increased strength.

PROPER FORM

Focus on the proper motion of the exercise, while concentrating on the specific muscles being used. Do not sacrifice proper form to lift heavier weight or perform more repetitions.

REST INTERVAL

Allow a brief pause between sets to give the muscles a chance to partially recover before working them again. For hypertrophy or muscle size development allow 1 to 1.5 minutes; for endurance allow 30 to 60 seconds; and for strength allow 3-4 minutes.

BREATHING

Never hold your breath during any part of an exercise. Holding your breath may cause severe intra-thoracic pressure and raise blood pressure leading to dizziness, blackout or other complications. The rule of thumb is to exhale on exertion and inhale on the return part of the exercise.

3. EXERCISE ORDER

When designing a strength training routine, always try to work the larger muscle groups first. Exercises that involve more than one muscle group (compound exercises) should be at the beginning of the routine and exercises that involve only one muscle group (isolation exercises) should follow. This will prevent your muscles from becoming prematurely tired.

Order of Muscle Groups by size for:
1) Upper Body
2) Lower Body
3) Core

Upper Body
- Chest (pectoralis major and pectoralis minor)
- Upper back (latissimus dorsi and rhomboids)
- Shoulders (anterior, medial, and posterior deltoids and trapezius)
- Rotator cuff (supraspinatus, infraspinous, teres major and minor, and subscapularis)
- Triceps (long, medium, and short heads)
- Biceps (biceps brachii, brachialis, brachioradialis)
- Forearms (flexors and extensors)

Lower Body
- Gluteal muscle group (buttocks)
- Hip muscle group (psoas, adductors, and abductors)
- Quadriceps muscle group (vastus medialis, vastus lateralis, vastus intermedius, and rectus femoris)
- Hamstrings muscle group (semimembranosus, semitendinosus, and biceps femoris)
- Calf muscle group (soleus, gastrocnemius, anterior tibialis)

(Core Group of Muscles) also known as the "Core"
Abdominals and Lower Back
- Abdominals (transverse and rectus abdominis, and obliques)
- Lower back (quadratus lumborum and erector spinae)

4. DESIGN YOUR PROGRAM

Go through each of the body sections in the exercise description section and pick out one to two exercises per body part. Write these exercises in your training diary or on a piece of paper. Mark next to each exercise the number of repetitions and sets you want to do and the workload or amount of weight to be lifted.

EXERCISES	REPETITIONS	SETS	WORKLOAD*
Lunges	8-12	3	moderate
Calf Raises	8-12	3	moderate
Bench Press	8-12	3	moderate
Bent-Over Row	8-12	3	moderate
Upright Row	8-12	3	moderate
Shoulder Press	8-12	3	moderate
Tricep Kickback	8-12	3	moderate
Alternating Bicep Curl	8-12	3	moderate
Wrist Curl	8-12	3	moderate
Reverse Wrist Curl	8-12	3	moderate
Abdominal Crunch	20-30	3	body weight

SAMPLE ROUTINE

The goal is to fatigue your muscles within the last few repetitions of the second and third set. If you are able to perform all three sets, while maintaining proper form, move onto a heavier weight.

*If you are a beginner, a three week pre-routine schedule is recommended. For the first week simply perform the exercises with very light weights such as a 1 lb or 2 lbs. This will help you to develop proper form. Coordination is developed in the second and third week, as you add a few pounds to each exercise. Once the three weeks have ended, begin adding more weight each week until you are barely capable of performing the required number of repetitions. The desired objective is to lift as much weight as possible, in a controlled movement, for the appropriate number of repetitions. In other words, challenge your body by increasing the workload as the exercises become easier.

STRETCHING

BY NIKOS APOSTOLOPOULOS, BPHE, NCCP-L3, AACA, AAA, ACSM, IASP

The two main purposes of stretching are prevention of injury caused by exercise or day-to-day activities and a faster rate of recovery from exercise. A regular stretching program will loosen muscle tissue, allowing an increased range of motion, which in turn helps prevent microtears at the muscle-tendon junction. Almost 90% of all injuries from muscle strain occur at the muscle-tendon junction and repeated injury at this junction leads to a build-up of scar tissue which impedes range of motion, adding stress on the joints. The sooner waste products from exercise (lactic acid) are removed from the muscle tissue, the sooner the muscle begins to heal. Stretching not only speeds removal of waste but increases the muscle's ability to bring in more nutrients. Keeping the muscles and tendons loose results in an increased range of motion, which helps to maintain the integrity of the joints.

Benefits of regular stretching

- decreased risk of injury from exercise
- increased range of motion and overall flexibility
- increased rate of recovery from exercise
- increase in strength (studies have shown that after a muscle has been stretched it recruits more fibres to perform a given task.)
- faster removal of waste products

Nikos Apostolopoulos is the founder of Stretch Therapy®, and microStretching®. He is the director of the Serapis Stretch Therapy Clinic in Vancouver, British Columbia, Canada, the only clinic in the world pioneering the development of therapeutic stretching. The clinic uses Stretch Therapy and microStretching--recovery regeneration techniques based on functional clinical anatomy--to treat many professional, elite and amateur athletes and individuals suffering from various musculoskeletal disorders.

Nikos graduated from the Faculty of Physical and Health Education at the University of Toronto with an emphasis in Sports Medicine. He has over 20 years experience in gross and functional anatomy and is a member of the American Association of Anatomists (AAA), American Association of Clinical Anatomists (AACA), American College of Sports Medicine (ACSM), and the International Association for the Study of Pain. He is currently working on his book MicroStretching-A New Approach.

Principles of Stretching

Try to set up a daily stretch routine; adhering to a consistent stretch program can have a profound impact on how you feel on a day-to-day basis. Moreover, if you stretch on a daily basis you can forgo the required pre-workout stretch. Please note: a warm-up prior to exercise is still required.

The problem with some traditional stretches is the muscle you are trying to stretch is the same muscle used to provide stability and balance. You can't stretch a muscle that is already in use. You'll notice many of the following stretches involve a chair, bench or wall to help isolate the target muscle group. By offering a base of support, the muscle group can be completely relaxed before the stretch.

HOW AND WHEN TO STRETCH

Frequency:	Try to stretch every day; do each stretch 3 times per muscle.
Intensity:	Light pressure, about 30-40% of max.
Duration:	Hold each stretch for 60 seconds: <u>Not more than 90 seconds.</u>

If you are unable to stretch on a daily basis, a pre and post-workout stretch is necessary. After a warm-up, but before the workout, do each of the 12 stretches twice, and after the workout one more time, for a total of three reps for each stretch.

Stretch Routine

(Follow the stretches in sequence)

1 Gastrocnemius Stretch

2 Soleus Stretch

- Keep the front knee slightly bent and the back knee straight with the heel down.
- Lean forward from the hips.
- Repeat with the other leg.

- Keep both knees slightly bent.
- Lean forward from the hips.
- Keep your heels on the floor.
- Repeat with the other leg.

③ Glute Stretch

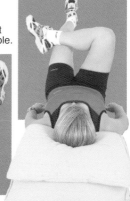

- Your right foot should be placed against the wall so that the right knee is as close to 90 degrees as is comfortable.
- Place your left ankle just past the right knee.
- Make sure the pelvis/hip area is not floating in the air; keep it as close to the floor as possible.
- Keep your shoulders on the floor.
- Repeat on the other side.

④ Hamstring Stretch

- Best performed on a corner wall so that one leg is up and the other straight.
- Keep the knee of your leg on the wall slightly bent (do not force straight).
- Keep your hips and pelvis square.
- If you feel a pull in the pelvis/abdominal area place a pillow under the knee of the straight leg.
- Repeat with the other leg.

⑤ Groin Stretch

- Make sure both upper and lower back are flat against the wall.
- Keep shoulders level and square.
- Do not force the groin muscles to be stretched.

⑥ Piriformis Stretch

- Try to keep shoulders and pelvis/hips on the floor.
- Place your right foot on the opposite side of the left knee.
- Gently pull your knee toward the floor with your left arm.
- Repeat on the other side.
- If you have difficulty reaching your knee, place more
  pillows behind the neck and shoulders.

⑦ Outer Leg Stretch

- Try to keep shoulders and pelvis/hips on floor.
- Bring left foot up to rest on the right knee.
- Your left thigh should be at 90 degrees to upper body.
- Gently pull your knee toward the floor with your right arm.
- Repeat on the other side.
- If you have difficulty reaching knee, place more pillows
  behind the neck and shoulders

⑧ Hip Flexor Stretch

- Make sure both hips and pelvis are square.
- Do not let your front knee go beyond 90 degrees.
- Try to keep lower back and upper body straight.
- Repeat with other leg forward.

(Alternative for people with bad knees)

⑨ Lower Back Stretch

- Keep your toes, ankles, and knees together.
- Bring your knees up until they are 90 degrees with the upper body.
- Slowly move your top shoulder back while trying to keep the knees together.
- Repeat on the other side.

⑩ Tricep/Rhomboids/ Rear Deltoids Stretch

- Make sure your shoulders are square and down.
- Slowly and gently pull your arm across the front of your body.
- Try to keep the lower back and upper body straight.

⑪ Upper Deltoid Stretch

- Behind your back, grasp your left elbow with the right hand.
- Keep the shoulders down.
- Do not force this stretch.
- Repeat on the other side.

⑫ Chest/Anterior Deltoid Stretch

- Place a hand on the wall so that your arm is down and slightly behind your back.
- Make sure the shoulders are square and down.
- Place your feet shoulder-width apart.
- Gently twist your body away from the arm on the wall.

Side View   Back View

DUMBBELL
EXERCISES

Upright Row

Muscles Worked
Upper Trapezius, Brachialis, Deltoid

START

FINISH

1. Stand with your feet comfortably spaced apart.
2. Bend your knees slightly.
3. Hold both dumbbells in front of your body so that the palms face toward you.
4. Begin lifting upward, keeping the dumbbells parallel to the floor.
5. Continue lifting to the mid chest line, pause for a moment, then slowly lower back to the starting position.

Warning: do not lift the dumbbells higher than mid chest as it may cause shoulder strain and/or damage.

Shoulders

Shoulder Press

Muscles Worked
Deltoids, Trapezius, Triceps

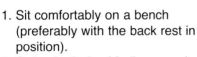

START

FINISH

1. Sit comfortably on a bench (preferably with the back rest in position).
2. Swing both dumbbells upward, to the starting position, so they are on either side of your head with your palms facing outward.
3. Slowly begin to push the dumbbells upward while keeping your elbows turned outward.
4. Do not lock your elbows or arch your back in the upper position. Keep your head level to the floor.
5. Pause briefly in the upper position, then slowly lower back to the starting position.

Standing Side Raise

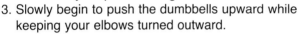

Muscles Worked
Deltoids, Upper Trapezius

START

FINISH

1. Stand with your feet comfortably spaced apart.
2. Bend your knees slightly.
3. With the dumbbells directly at your sides, begin to lift them away from your body in an upward and outward motion.
4. Bring your arms up until they reach shoulder level.
5. Hold this position for a moment and then slowly lower the dumbbells back down to the beginning position.

Shoulder Shrug

Muscles Worked

Upper Trapezius,
Levator Scapulae

START

FINISH

1. Stand upright, knees slightly bent, and your feet comfortably spaced apart.
2. Bend your knees slightly.
3. With the dumbbells directly at your sides, slowly raise your shoulders toward your ears.
4. Keep your arms straight and do not arch your back in an effort to lift the dumbbells higher.
5. Pause in the upper position for a moment, then slowly lower the dumbbells back down.

ADVANCED

START

FINISH

Same as above but lean forward 30 degrees and lift your shoulders toward the ceiling.

Shoulders

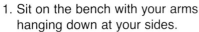

Seated Incline Deltoid Raise

Muscles Worked

Anterior Deltoid, Coracobrachialis

START

FINISH

1. Sit on the bench with your arms hanging down at your sides.
2. Your palms should be facing inward.
3. Keeping your elbows slightly bent, rotate the dumbbells inward as you raise them to chest level. The dumbbells should be parallel to the floor.
4. Pause briefly in the finish position, then lower back to the starting point.

Note: For a challenge, keep your head on the bench without hyper-extending the neck.

Screwdriver

Muscles Worked

Infraspinatus, Teres Minor, Posterior Deltoid

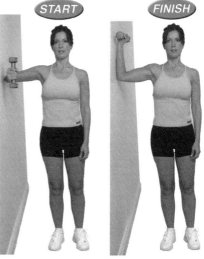

START

FINISH

1. Standing sideways to the wall, place your elbow on the wall so that your upper arm is parallel to the floor.
2. Rotate the dumbbell backwards, without dislodging your elbow from the wall.
3. Imagine your elbow is screwing a bolt into the wall.
4. Pause briefly in the finish position, then return to the start.
5. Don't move any other part of the body, except the working arm.

Shoulders

Pec Minor Punch

Muscles Worked
Pectoralis Minor, Serratus Anterior

1. Lie on your back with your arms pointing straight up to the ceiling.
2. Your palms should be facing each other.
3. Start with your shoulder blades against the floor.
4. Slowly, punch the dumbbells upward; pushing your shoulder blades toward the ceiling.
5. Pause briefly in the top position, then lower to start position.

The return phase of an exercise is as important as the execution. The return should be slow and controlled.

Lying Single Arm Flyes

Muscles Worked
Posterior Deltoid, Middle Trapezius, Rhomboids

START

FINISH

1. Lie sideways on a bench, with your bottom arm braced on the floor. Keep your neck in a neutral alignment.
2. Holding a dumbbell, start with your top arm pointing toward the floor; the elbow is slightly bent.
3. Maintaining a stiff elbow joint, raise your top arm up until it is just beyond parallel to the floor. Keep your wrist straight through the motion.
4. Pause briefly in the finish position, then slowly lower to the start position.

Standing Bent–Over Flyes

Muscles Worked

Posterior Deltoid, Middle Trapezius, Rhomboids

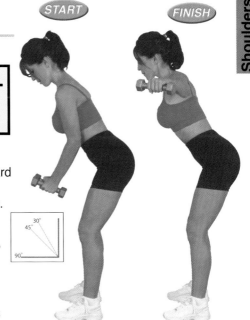

1. From a standing position, bend forward from the hips to a 30–45 degree angle. Keep your head in neutral alignment.
2. Maintain a "butt-out" arch with the lower back throughout the movement.
3. Start with your arms in the lower position–the elbows slightly bent.
4. Raise your arms up until they are parallel to the floor–keep the wrists straight.
5. Pause briefly in the finish position, then slowly lower to the start position.

ALTERNATIVE

Note: Advanced individuals can try this exercise at 45–90 degree angles of forward bend.

Bent-Over Flattener

Warning: This is an advanced exercise. Use no weight when attempting this exercise for the first time. When you feel comfortable with the movement, try a pair of very light dumbbells.

Muscles Worked

Posterior Deltoid,
Middle Deltoid,
Trapezius

START

FINISH

1. From a standing position, bend forward from the hips to a 30–45 degree angle. Keep your head in neutral alignment.
2. Start with your arms at shoulder level, the elbows bent to 90 degree angles and your palms facing each other.
3. Throughout the movement, maintain a "butt-out" arch with your lower back.
4. Start by pressing your arms up and out at a 45 degree angle.
5. Pause briefly in the finish position, when your elbows are straight.
6. Slowly, bring your arms back to the starting position.

Alternating Front Deltoid Raise

Muscles Worked
Anterior Deltoid, Coracobrachialis

START *FINISH*

1. Stand with your feet comfortably spaced apart.
2. Bend your knees slightly.
3. With the dumbbells directly at your sides, begin to lift the right arm away from your body in an upward and forward motion.
4. Bring your arm up until it reaches shoulder level.
5. Hold this position for a moment and then slowly lower the dumbbell back down to the beginning position.
6. Repeat on the other side.

Alternative: Raise both dumbbells at the same time, being careful not to arch your back. <u>This exercise involves more back stabilization</u>.

ALTERNATIVE

Side Lying Neutral (with towel)

Muscles Worked
Infraspinatus,
Teres Minor

Rotator Cuff

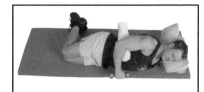

START

FINISH

1. Lie on your side with a towel between your elbow and waist. Place a pillow under your head to maintain neutral neck alignment.
2. Grip a dumbbell with the hand of your top arm.
3. Bend the elbow of your top arm to 90 degrees and keep your wrist straight.
4. Start with the dumbbell toward the floor and your forearm across your stomach.
5. Squeeze down on the towel against your waist. Maintain this pressure throughout the exercise.
6. Slowly raise the dumbbell, until your forearm is parallel to the floor.
7. Pause briefly in the finish position, then slowly lower to the start position.

Note: Avoid movement of the shoulder blade; keep your wrist fixed throughout the movement.

Physio Note: The pressure against the towel helps to secure the head of the Humerus in the Glenoid Fossa (shoulder socket).

Side Lying with Arm Braced

Muscles Worked
Infraspinatus,
Teres Minor

Rotator Cuff

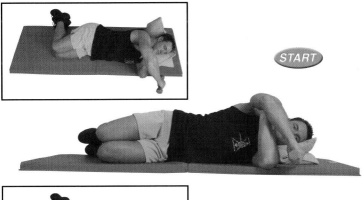

START

FINISH

1. Lie on your side with a pillow under your head to maintain neutral neck alignment. Pick up a dumbbell with the hand of your top arm.
2. Hold onto your top arm, just above the elbow, with the hand of your lower arm (fingers over top of your bicep; thumb under).
3. Position your upper arm parallel to the floor and at a 90 degree angle between the hips and head.
4. Start with the dumbbell in the lower position.
5. Slowly raise the dumbbell, until your forearm is parallel to the floor, or slightly higher.
6. Pause briefly in the finish position, then slowly lower back to the start position.

Note: Change the arm angle to ensure shoulder strength and stability in a multitude of arm movement patterns.

Prone External Rotation

Muscles Worked
Infraspinatus, Teres Minor, Posterior Deltoid

Rotator Cuff

Warning: This is an advanced exercise. Use no weight when attempting this exercise for the first time. When you feel comfortable with the movement try a pair of very light dumbbells.

1. Lie face down on a bench with your head over the edge. Keep your neck in neutral alignment.
2. Position your upper arms parallel to the floor and at shoulder level.
3. Bend your elbows to 90 degrees.
4. Start with the dumbbells rotated downward to the lower position.
5. Without dropping your elbows, slowly raise the dumbbells until your forearms are parallel to the floor. Maintain the angle at your elbow throughout the exercise motion.
6. Pause briefly in the finish position, then slowly lower to the start position

Incline External Rotation

Muscles Worked
Infraspinatus, Teres Minor, Posterior Deltoid

Rotator Cuff

START

FINISH

1. Set the bench to a 30 degree incline position.
2. Sit facing the bench with your neck in a neutral alignment.
3. Position your upper arms parallel to the floor and at shoulder level.
4. Bend your elbows to 90 degrees and point your hands toward the floor.
5. Without dropping your elbows, slowly raise your hands until they are pointing toward the ceiling. Maintain the angle at your elbow throughout the exercise motion.
6. Pause briefly in the finish position, then slowly lower to the start position.

Note: This is a difficult exercise to do properly with weights. Do this exercise without weights until you have mastered the technique.

Bench Press

Muscles Worked
Pectoralis Major, Anterior Deltoid, Triceps

Chest

START

FINISH

1. Lie flat on a bench.
2. Begin this exercise with two dumbbells held above your shoulders, arms extended and elbows slightly flexed.
3. Place your feet on the bench to prevent your back from arching.
4. Slowly lower the dumbbells, with your elbows turned outward, until your arms are parallel to the floor.
5. Avoid dropping your elbows below bench level.
6. Pause in the lower position for a moment, then slowly raise the dumbbells back to the starting position.

Lying Pullover

Muscles Worked

Pectoralis Major,
Latissimus Dorsi

Chest

START

FINISH

1. Lie flat on a bench holding a single dumbbell in both hands with the palms facing upward and thumbs around the dumbbell handles, directly above your chest.
2. Without arching your lower back, slowly lower the dumbbell behind your head, until you feel a comfortable stretch.
3. Hold for a second, then slowly bring your arms back to the original position.
4. Make sure the motion is well controlled throughout the exercise.

Flyes

Muscles Worked

Pectoralis Major,
Anterior Deltoid

Chest

START

FINISH

1. Lie flat on the bench holding a dumbbell in each hand.
2. Begin with your arms straight up in front of you so that your palms face each other.
3. Slowly lower the dumbbells to your sides in a circular fashion, bending your elbows slightly as you come down (this helps take pressure off your shoulder muscles).
4. Once in the lowered position, hold for a second, then raise the dumbbells in the same fashion, while squeezing your chest (Movement resembles hugging a tree).
5. Keep the movement smooth and concentrate on working your chest, not your arms or shoulders.

Bent-Over Lateral

Muscles Worked
Middle Trapezius, Posterior Deltoids, Rhomboids

START

FINISH

1. Sitting on the edge of a bench, lean forward.
2. Start by holding both dumbbells next to your ankles with your palms facing each other.
3. Slowly begin to pull the dumbbells outward and upward in a semi-circular motion until your arms reach shoulder height.
4. Keep your head in a neutral position, eyes looking at the floor and your elbows fixed with a slight bend.
5. Hold in the upper position for a moment, then slowly lower the dumbbells back to the starting position.

Bent-Over Row

Muscles Worked
Latissimus Dorsi, Rhomboids, Posterior Deltoids

Back

START

FINISH

1. Grip a dumbbell in your left hand.
2. Place your right knee and right hand on the bench.
3. Keep your left knee slightly bent and your back flat throughout the exercise.
4. Draw the dumbbell upward toward the lower ribs, keeping your elbow close to your body on the way up.
5. Pause in the upper position for a moment, then slowly lower the dumbbell back down until your arm is fully extended.
6. Perform a set on the left side, then switch to your right side.

Deadlift

Muscles Worked
Erector Spinae, Hamstrings, Gluteus Maximus

START

FINISH

Back

1. Stand upright, knees slightly bent and your feet comfortably spaced apart.
2. With the dumbbells directly in front of you, slowly bend forward from the hips lowering the dumbbells toward the floor.
3. Bend slightly at the knees and keep the dumbbells close to your legs as you go down and come back up.
4. Keep your head neck and back in line and your arms straight throughout the exercise.
5. Pause at the bottom and slowly return to the standing position, straightening your legs and hips at the same time.
6. When performing this exercise for the first time, use little or no weight as there is a possibility of lower back strain.

Note: Don't look up.

Alternating Hammer Curl

START

Muscles Worked
Biceps,
Brachioradialis,
Brachialis

FINISH

Biceps

ALTERNATIVE

1. Sit comfortably on a bench, preferably with the back support upright.
2. Hold the dumbbells at your sides with your palms facing inward.
3. With your upper arm in a fixed position, lift the dumbbell upward, keeping your palm inward throughout the complete range of motion.
4. Lift and lower one dumbbell, then the other.
5. Keep your elbow in tight to your ribs.
6. Make sure your motions are slow and controlled; do not use momentum to perform this exercise.

Alternative: Raise both dumbbells at the same time, making sure not to arch your back to complete the movement. This exercise increases the intensity and saves time.

Standing Bicep Curl

Muscles Worked

Biceps, Brachialis, Brachioradialis

START

FINISH

Biceps

1. Stand upright, knees slightly bent, and your feet comfortably spaced apart.
2. With the dumbbells directly in front of you, palms facing away, begin to lift both weights up toward your shoulders, keeping your upper arms fixed.
3. If you are arching your back in an effort to lift the dumbbells, use a lighter weight.
4. Once in the upper position hold for a second, then slowly lower the dumbbells back down until your arms are fully extended.

Incline Bicep Curl

Muscles Worked
Biceps, Brachialis, Brachioradialis

Biceps

START

FINISH

ALTERNATIVE

1. Set the bench to an incline position.
2. Start by sitting on the bench with your head against the back rest and your arms hanging down at your side.
3. Palms are face up and dumbbells pointing sideways.
4. Keeping the upper arm stable, raise the dumbbells to chest level.
5. Pause briefly in the top position then slowly lower back to the starting point.

Alternative: If your neck is uncomfortable or hyper-extending, bring your head forward off the bench.

Concentration Curl

Muscles Worked
Biceps, Brachialis, Brachioradialis

START

1. Sit comfortably on a bench with your feet spread slightly wider than shoulder width apart.
2. Lean over until your left elbow is placed to the inside of your left thigh, just above your knee.
3. Your left arm should be hanging vertical, holding the dumbbell, while your right hand is on your right knee for support.
4. Curl your arm upward, raising the dumbbell, while holding your leg and elbow in place.
5. The dumbbell should move toward your upper right chest.
6. Keep your head up, back straight, and avoid dropping your shoulder to lift the weight.
7. Slowly lower and repeat.
8. Complete the set on one side then switch.

FINISH

Biceps

Incline One-Arm Preacher Curl

Muscles Worked
Biceps, Brachialis, Brachioradialis

START

1. Set the bench to an incline position. Grip a dumbbell in your right hand.
2. Standing behind the bench, place your upper arm on the backrest.
3. Curl your arm upward, raising the dumbbell, while holding your upper arm in place.
4. The dumbbell should move toward your right shoulder. Pause when you feel a good contraction in your bicep.
5. Hold this position for a moment and then slowly lower the dumbbell back down.

FINISH

Seated Tricep Press

Muscles Worked

Triceps

START

FINISH

Triceps

1. Sit on the end of the bench with your feet comfortably spaced apart.
2. Hold the dumbbell overhead with both hands, palms facing upward and thumbs around the dumbbell handles.
3. Inhale while slowly lowering the dumbbell behind your head until your forearms come in contact with your biceps.
4. Keep your head up, back straight and hold your elbows in close to your head.
5. Exhale and extend your elbows until your arms are straight.
6. Make sure the motion is completely controlled.

Kickback

Muscles Worked

Triceps

START

FINISH

1. Lean over the bench, putting your left knee and left palm on the bench top.
2. With your right hand grip the dumbbell. Your back and upper right arm should be parallel to the bench.
3. Hold your elbow in tight to your side and straighten your elbow so that your entire arm becomes parallel to the floor. Avoid twisting to lift the dumbbell higher.
4. Hold for a second then slowly return.
5. Remember to keep your upper arm fixed during the entire motion.
6. Complete the set, then repeat with your left arm.

Overhead Tricep Press

Muscles Worked

Triceps

Triceps

1. Lie flat on the bench with a dumbbell in each hand.
2. Begin with your arms straight up in front of you so that your palms face each other.
3. Keeping your elbows fixed in place, slowly lower the dumbbells toward either side of your head until your forearms are parallel to the floor.
4. Hold for a second then slowly return.
5. Remember to keep your elbows fixed during the entire motion.

Wrist Curl

START

Muscles Worked
**Wrist Flexors,
Finger Flexors**

1. Sit comfortably on a bench with your feet spread slightly wider than shoulder width apart.
2. Grip a dumbbell in your left hand.
3. Support your forearm by placing it on your thigh so that the wrist joint is at the edge of your knee and your palm is facing upward.
4. Relax your wrist so that the dumbbell is in the lower position. FINISH
5. Curl the dumbbell upward with your hand until your wrist is completely flexed. Your elbow and forearm should remain in contact with your thigh throughout the exercise.
6. Slowly lower the dumbbell back to the start position.
7. Repeat on other side

Reverse Wrist Curl

Muscles Worked
Wrist Extensors

START

1. Sit comfortably on a bench with your feet spread slightly wider than shoulder width apart.
2. Grip a dumbbell in your left hand.
3. Support your forearm by placing it on your thigh so that the wrist joint is at the edge of your knee and your palm is facing downward.
4. Relax your wrist so that the dumbbell is in the lower position.
5. Curl the dumbbell upward with your hand until your wrist is completely extended. Your elbow and forearm should remain in contact with your thigh throughout the exercise.
6. Slowly lower the dumbbell back to the start position. FINISH
7. Repeat on other side

Forearms

Squat

Muscles Worked

Quadriceps, Gluteus Maximus,
Hamstrings, Erector Spinae

START

FINISH

Legs

1. While gripping the head of a dumbbell with both hands, stand so that your feet are shoulder width apart and toes are turned out 20–45 degrees.
2. Bend your knees slightly and keep your head level to the floor throughout the exercise.
3. With the dumbbell hanging directly in front of you, lower your hips until your upper thighs are almost parallel to the floor.
4. Do not bend your front knee beyond 90 degrees (beyond your toes).
5. Pause at the bottom and slowly return to the standing position, straightening your legs and hips at the same time.
6. Keep your back flat or with a slight arch, throughout the exercise.
7. Keep your feet firmly on the floor and squat only as low as you can with proper technique. Use little or no weight the first time you perform this exercise.

See-Wall Squat

Muscles Worked

Quadriceps, Gluteus Maximus, Hamstrings, Erector Spinae

START

FINISH

• One way to ensure proper technique when doing a squat is to stand facing a wall. This forces you to be aware of moving straight up and down.

1. Stand facing the wall, so that your toes are 3 inches from the wall. Your feet are shoulder width apart and toes are turned out slightly.
2. Place the dumbbells on the muscles of the shoulders.
3. Squat down; avoid touching the wall or rounding the back
4. Maintain a "butt-out" arch with the lower back throughout the movement. Keep your head leveled with the floor.
5. Pause briefly in the lower position, return to the start position.

Legs

Note: Keep your head up and chest out.

Split Squat

Muscles Worked

Quadriceps,
Gluteus Maximus,
Hamstrings

START

FINISH

Legs

1. Stand with your feet spaced about 3–4 feet apart, one in front of the other.
2. Keep your back straight and head level to the floor throughout this exercise.
3. Slowly drop your hips toward the floor until your back knee nearly touches the floor.
4. Pause for a moment in the lower position, then slowly push yourself back to the start position. On the next set repeat with the other leg forward.
5. Do not bend the front of your knee beyond the front of your toes.

Lunge

Muscles Worked

Quadriceps,
Gluteus Maximus,
Hamstrings

START

FINISH

Warning: This is an advanced exercise. Use no weight when attempting this exercise for the first time. When you feel comfortable with the movement try a pair of very light dumbbells.

1. Stand with your feet slightly apart. Keep your back straight and your head level to the floor throughout this exercise.
2. Step forward about 3–4 feet with your right foot, planting it firmly on the floor.
3. Drop your hips until your back knee nearly touches the floor.
4. Pause for a moment, then push yourself back into starting position. Repeat with the other leg.
5. Do not bend your front knee beyond 90 degrees (beyond your toes).

Legs

Note: This is an advanced exercise and beginners should start with the "Split Squat" until they feel comfortable with the motion.

Side Squat Lunge

Muscles Worked
Quadriceps, Adductors, Hamstrings, Gluteus Maximus

START

FINISH

Legs

1. Stand with your arms at your side and dumbbells on your upper thighs.
2. Without moving your feet, squat sideways, keeping one leg straight and bending the knee of the other, keep your head in neutral alignment.
3. Maintain a "butt-out" arch with the lower back throughout the movement.
4. Move your knee in the direction of the toes.
5. Pause briefly in the lower position, then return to the starting point.

Seated Calf Raise

Muscles Worked
Soleus

START

FINISH

1. Place a dumbbell on the floor to the right side of the bench so that when you sit down, the dumbbell is directly in front of your right foot.
2. Place the ball of your right foot on the handle of the dumbbell with your knee bent to 90 degrees.
3. Hold another dumbbell on your right thigh about 2 inches back from your knee cap.
4. Slowly raise your right knee up, by pushing down with your toes and lifting your heel off the floor.
5. Hold in the upper position for a second and then lower the heel.
6. Perform a set on the right side then switch to the right.

Legs

Warning: If you find the dumbbell on the floor to be unstable, try placing a heavier dumbbell on the floor or secure the other side of the dumbbell with your other foot.

Standing Calf Raise	Muscles Worked
	Gastrocnemius

START

FINISH

Legs

1. Place a platform (with a height of approximately 6 inches) that will allow a full range of motion at the ankle, next to the bench.
2. Grip a dumbbell in your left hand.
3. Using a bench in the upright position for support, stand on a well supported platform on the ball of your left foot. The arch and heel should be over the edge of the platform.
4. Slowly rise up on your tiptoes, keeping your head level to the floor and back straight.
5. Pause briefly at the top and slowly come back down.
6. Repeat on the other side.

**Walking
Heel Raise**

Muscles Worked

Gastrocnemius, Soleus,
Tibialis Posterior, Peroneals

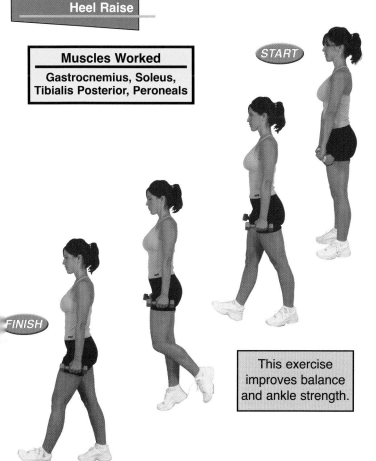

START

FINISH

This exercise
improves balance
and ankle strength.

1. Stand with a pair of dumbbells hanging at your sides,
2. Step forward with your right foot placing the heel onto the floor first.
3. Raise up onto the toes of the right foot. Pause briefly in this position, maintaining your balance.
4. Still up on your toes of the right foot, begin bringing your left foot forward and placing the heel onto the floor first as you lower your right foot to the floor again.
5. Repeat this process with the other foot and continue walking in this manner.

Legs

**Note: Hold the pause at the top to maximize
your training benefits.**

Standing Hip Flexor

Legs

1. Stand holding a dumbbell (or two) in your right hand.
2. Step forward slightly with the left foot and place the dumbbell on the thigh of the left leg.
3. Raise your left knee until the leg is parallel to the floor.
4. Pause briefly, then return to the starting point.
5. Perform a set on one side then switch to the other.

Note: Maintain an upright, firm posture throughout the movement.

Two-Arm Dumbbell Crunch

Muscles Worked
Rectus Abdominis

1. Lie on a mat with your knees bent.
2. Grip a dumbbell with both hands.
3. Hold the dumbbell above your head with your arms straight up.
4. Crunch up, trying to push the dumbbell straight up toward the ceiling.
5. The motion should come from the contraction of your abdominal muscles.
6. Pause in the upper position, then return to the floor.

Note: Maintain a neutral neck alignment and don't hold your breath.

Core

One-Arm Dumbbell Crunch

Muscles Worked
Obliques

START

FINISH

1. Lie on a mat with your knees bent.
2. Grip a dumbbell in one hand.
3. Hold the dumbbell above your head so that your arm is straight and pointing up to the ceiling.
4. Crunch up and try to push the dumbbell straight up to the ceiling.
5. The motion should come from the contraction of your abdominal muscles.
6. Pause in the top position, then return to the floor.

Core

Note: Maintain a neutral neck alignment and don't hold your breath.

Bridge with Dumbbell

Muscles Worked
Erector Spinae, Hamstrings, Gluteus Maximus

START

FINISH

ADVANCED

1. Lie on a mat with your knees bent.
2. Grip a dumbbell with both hands and place it on your lower abdomen. Continue gripping the dumbbell.
3. Bring your hips off the floor until your knees are at a 90degree bend and your torso is perfectly straight.
4. Pause in this position, then slowly lower your hips back to the floor.

Note: Advanced individuals can try this exercise on one leg.

Core

Reverse Leg Lift

Muscles Worked
Erector Spinae, Hamstrings, Gluteus Maximus

START

FINISH

ALTERNATIVE

1. Lie face down on the bench with your hips hanging off the edge of the bench.
2. Hold onto the end of the bench, while raising both heels off the floor.
3. Raise the heels up until your body is straight (beginners should use one leg).
4. Pause briefly in the top position, then return to the starting position.

Alternative: Place a weighted object on the other end if the bench does not remain on the floor.

Core

Pointing Dog

Muscles Worked
Erector Spinae, Hamstrings, Gluteus Maximus

START

FINISH

BEGINNER

1. Grip a dumbbell in your right hand.
2. Kneel forward on your right knee while supporting yourself with your left arm.
3. Keep your head and spine in a neutral alignment.
4. Raise the dumbbell forward while extending your left leg behind you.
5. Pause in the upper position, then return to the starting position.
6. Repeat on the other side.

Note: Should this exercise cause you pain, please see your physician.

Core

Other products by
Productive Fitness Products Inc.

The Great Handbook Series
Canada $10.95   U.S. $8.95

The Great Handbooks Series are a wonderful addition to your exercise library. These books have all the different exercises you need for working your whole body. In addition, they discuss how to set up a program, how to stretch, how to stay motivated, and safety tips. All have 64 pages of exercises using popular pieces of fitness equipment. The books, sold separately, are written and edited by experts in a clear and concise manner, with step-by-step instructions and full color photos for all exercises.

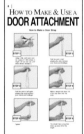

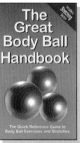

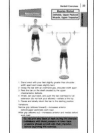

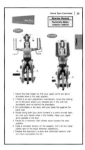

The Ultimate Weight Training Journal

More than a _one-year personal fitness diary_, The Ultimate Weight Training Journal discusses basic nutrition, aerobics, and strength training. But best of all, this book shows you how these three tools can best be used in attaining a better physique, better health, and more strength.

288 pages

One Year of Training Log pages based on 3-4 workouts per week.

Canada $18.95
U.S. $14.95

Poster Packs
Canada $29.95   U.S. $22.95

These full-color, laminated posters will make your workouts more effective by allowing you to quickly identify proper exercise form and technique. Sold in sets of four or five posters, each set sells for $29.95 (Cdn) $22.95 (U.S.)

Dumbbell Training Poster Pack
- Four Full-Color 12" x 18" Posters -

Body Ball Training Poster Pack
- Four Full-Color 12" x 18" Posters -

Stretch Tubing Training Poster Pack
- Five Full-Color 12" x 18" Posters -